Quench

*30-day devotional for those thirsty in
body, mind & spirit*

Ashley Hall Roberts

DEDICATION

Dedicated to my Lord and Savior, Jesus Christ, who has shown me just how much He desires to have **all** of me devoted to Him – body, mind and spirit.

And to my family and friends who have inspired, supported and encouraged me on this amazing journey!

"I lift my hands to You in prayer. I thirst for You as parched land thirsts for water."

Psalm 143:6

CONTENTS

INTRODUCTION

What if we are only touching a portion of our power?
What if we are only realizing a fraction of the abundant life
that Jesus promised us? What if we are standing in our
own way of experiencing God more fully in our daily lives?

If we look hard and deep within, most of us know this is
probably true. We live in a world that lures us into being
divided against ourselves. Even our modern faith practices
tend to keep us divided against ourselves.

What if you were united in body, mind and spirit?
The Father, Son and Spirit are united in purpose and
power. What might happen if you, like the Godhead, had
all three parts of yourself united in purpose and power --
integrated in body, mind and spirit?

Let's begin to find out ....

DAY 1: BODY AS SACRED

"Do you not know that your bodies are temples of the Holy Spirit, who is in you, whom you have received from God? You are not your own; you were bought with a price. Therefore honor God with your bodies." I Corinthians 6:19-20 (NIV)

As a Christ-follower, I have heard numerous sermons on this verse over the years. Almost all of them have been about one of three things: sexual impurity, addiction or, perhaps, self-mutilation.

While I whole-heartedly agree that God doesn't desire those three things for us or our bodies, I also believe He has so much more in mind.
What if we began a dialogue about treating our bodies as something beautiful and holy that God created? (Which, of course, He did). What if we began to care for our bodies in kind, caring & respectful ways? What if we thought about fueling it properly, strengthening and growing it to its fuller potential, and ensuring it received the rest

1

that it needs? What if we began to see our bodies as one of the most amazing gifts that God has given us and began to steward it accordingly?

I think it's time to reclaim our bodies as something sacred. How about you?

DAY 2: YOU

"So our aim is to please Him always, whether we
are here in this body or away from this body."
2 Corinthians 5:9 (NLT)

Who are you? If I were to ask you that, you would
probably start offering a list of adjectives describing
yourself. Some of those adjectives would describe
your personality, like and dislikes, etc. Others
might include physical descriptors such as tall,
brunette, pretty, whatever. It's only natural, right?
It's part of who we are.

Or is it?

Part of what Paul is discussing here in his second
letter to the church of Corinth is that God has
prepared a new body for us in heaven -- an eternal
body. We will leave these "earthly tents" (v. 1) when
we die, & we will put on a new heavenly body.
Anyone who has stood at the bedside of someone
who was dying has seen this reality in living color.

3

It stands to reason, then, that if you leave your body, your body is not you. You are something much more profound. You are you, something inside your body. And Your body is, instead, a vessel ... a container of you. Said differently, it is the container in which you live and move and have your being.

With that in mind, I would argue that your body is a gift -- an amazing, beautiful, complex gift that God has given you to steward during your lifetime. Yes, this body may pass away (as will money, time, resources, talents, etc.) -- but unlike all those other gifts (which, by the way, you spend a lot of energy stewarding), your body is with you your entire earthly journey.

God has given you a beautiful gift. It is **your** body to use throughout **your** entire earthly journey. It is the vessel in which **you** live and move and have your being. It is, arguably, your most precious gift. Every ministry act you ever make is made through it. Every act of kindness, charity, love or generosity is made through it. And only **you** can care for it and steward it well.

DAY 3: THE BODY

"For we know that ... when we die and leave this earthly body, we will have ... an eternal body made for us by God Himself .... [W]e will put on heavenly bodies; we will not be spirits without bodies." 2 Corinthians 5:1-3 (NLT)

Have you ever wondered if the body is important to God? Have you ever searched the Bible to see if the body mattered to God?

While I haven't yet made an exhaustive search of the Scriptures on this matter, here are a few of the clues I first discovered:
- God "formed a man's body from the dust of the ground and breathed into it the breath of life" (*Genesis 2:7*), and God made woman out of Adam's own body (*Genesis 2:22*). God Himself fashioned the human body, and He breathed His own breath into it. With great care and attention to detail, He made male and female interconnected in numerous ways.

- God made mankind in His own image (*Genesis 1:27*). The Scriptures tell us that God not only fashioned us with delicate care, but also that He made us in His own image. The way God made us – inclusive of our bodies – was such that we are like Him!!!
- When we die, we are given a new body; we are not simply spirit form in the afterlife, but with a new body. *(See also 1 Corinthians 15:40, 54; Romans 8:23.)* To me, this indicates the importance of a body from God's perspective. I cannot fully grasp His rationale, but the body must have significance. If our spirit/soul was all that mattered to God, why wouldn't we be purely spirit/soul in the afterlife? Instead, God grants us a new body.
- Followers of Jesus are called the "body of Christ" (*see e.g., 1 Corinthians 12:12-31, Romans 12:4-5, Ephesians 2:16*, etc.). While most consider this to be a metaphor, why would God choose this particular metaphor? God surely wouldn't have picked this metaphor if the body was insignificant and didn't matter to Him!
- Scripture says that a believer's body is "actually part of Christ" and is "the temple of the Holy Spirit" (*1 Corinthians 6:15, 19*). The reality of this is mind-blowing! Scripture tells us to honor God with our bodies (*1 Corinthians 6:20*). Enough said?

Each of these clues unquestionably reveal that the body God made for us is important. It matters to God. Yes, they body is passing away, but for whatever reasons, it remains important to Him.

Is it important to you?

DAY 4: SHEMA

"Hear o Israel: The LORD our God, the LORD is one. Love the LORD your God with all your heart and with all your soul and with all your strength." Deuteronomy 6:4-5 (NIV)

The SHEMA is an ancient Jewish prayer that is arguably one of the most important prayers in Judaism. It is recited in the morning and evening prayer services. It begins with *"Hear o Israel: the LORD our God, the LORD is one."*

As Christians (Judeo-Christians, to be specific), we have come to understand The Lord as three in one. God is one, and yet God is triune -- Father, Son and Spirit. There are three aspects, or three faces, of God ... yet God is still one.

I believe that one of the ways God made us in His image is that He made us triune. We too are one and yet triune -- body, mind and spirit. And God has asked us to worship and love Him with all of who we are. God desires for us to love Him with our heart and our soul and our strength -- with our complete triunity.

God didn't have to make us with a body. But He did. God doesn't have to give us a new body in the afterlife (why not let us be all spirit?), but He will. (*See e.g., Romans 8:23, 1 Corinthians 15:45-58, & 2 Corinthians 5:1-10*). For His reasons, God values the body. And he asks us to love Him with all that He made us to be.

Let us worship and adore God with this body -- starting here, starting now ... while we still can.

DAY 5: FLESH

"And the Word was made flesh and dwelt among us ...." John 1:14a (KJV)

In Christian parlance, the word "flesh" has gotten a bad rap. Most Christians associate "the flesh" with things sinful or evil or tempting. But the word used for "flesh" in the Bible actually carries no such connotation.

The Greek word "sarx" simply means "flesh" -- skin, meat, bones -- whether of men, beasts, fish or birds. It has neither a good nor a bad association with it. The New Living Translation of the Bible does a better job of keeping the word neutral, in its original sense.

So why & how did "flesh" get such a bad rap?

That's a long and complicated story, but for now, may God encourage you & renew your mind about how you think about your flesh.

Your flesh was created by God and given to you. It is a gift. It has amazing potential for good and for beauty and for reflecting God's glory. Your flesh is an integral part of how God made you. And He does not ask you to divide yourself against yourself. In God's kingdom, there is no separation between the sacred and the secular. God wants all of you. Can the flesh do bad things? Yes. And so can the mind. And so can the spirit. It's what we do or don't do with our flesh that constitutes something good or something evil. The flesh itself is not evil. After all, the Word became flesh. God Himself incarnate in the flesh ...

... and He did something wonderful with His. Will you?

DAY 6: ACT OF WORSHIP

"Therefore I urge you, brothers and sisters, in view of God's mercy, to offer your bodies as a living sacrifice, holy and pleasing to God -- that is your true and proper worship." Romans 12:1 (NIV)

Is it odd to you that the body – your body -- can be offered as an act of worship? That is exactly what this passage says – that offering our bodies as a living sacrifice is true and proper worship.

So often, the messages I have received from the Christian community is that the body is "flesh" ... meaning that is it evil and corrupt. Or if not that, I have the message at that our earthly bodies are insignificant to our relationship with God.

But I don't believe that is Biblical.

The Bible constantly reminds us that the human body is a beautiful and incredible instrument that God has made, given and entrusted to us. It is in and through this amazing body that anything and everything we do flows. And the way we care for our bodies can truly be an act of worship.

How? As with most things, it starts with a perspective shift.

In this passage, Paul urges us urges us to offer our bodies as a living sacrifice *"in view of God's mercy."* In other words, in light of all we have received in Christ and all that we receive through Christ every day, will you offer your body as a living sacrifice, holy and pleasing to Him.

(This is one of those passages that reveals so much about the heart of God: notice how God never asks us to do something without reminding us of what He has already done or will do for us.)

And Romans 12 continues: *"Do not be conformed to this world, but be transformed by the renewing of your mind."* We start with a perspective shift – a renewing of the mind -- then begins the work of integrating our renewed perspective into the daily way we do things. As with any new spiritual practice, it takes intentionality, focus and repetition at first, but it soon becomes second nature.

So first, ask God to help you renew your mind about the way you think about, interact with, and treat your body. God is able to renew and restore! Then, take a step of faith consistent with your renewed perspective. Consider how you **nourish** and **strengthen** and **care for** your body ... and consider it a spiritual act of worship. Because it is.

DAY 7: FOOD-SESSION

"Why pay money for something that will not nourish you? Why spend your hard-earned money on something that will not satisfy? Listen carefully to me and eat what is nourishing!"
 Isaiah 55:2 (NET)

Would you put maple syrup in your car instead of gasoline? "But it tastes better!" Maybe so, but the car won't run on maple syrup. In fact, you might end up ruining your car!

Look around. That's just what we (as a society) are doing. Filling our mouths with food that tastes good, but does not provide us with the nourishment we need. Food that ends up ruining the marvelous creation that God made.

Food was meant to be fuel for the body. Food was intended to serve the body and provide it what it needs for optimal performance. But our society has completely inverted that formula. For many, the body is at the mercy of food. We are food-obsessed. The pleasure of our taste-buds has taken first priority, and nutrition and nourishment have taken a back seat (heck, they may even have been tossed out of the car by now)!

Join me in the fight against this obsession with food (our "food-session," for short). Reclaim the body as God designed and intended. Reclaim food as fuel -- as nourishment for your body -- and not as the destroyer of God's good creation. Reclaim God's intended order that food is for the body not the other way around.

It's going to be a tough fight. I have a 9-year-old and a 7-year-old. I tell them often that we eat for our bodies, not for our mouths. On certain days, I have them look at "My Healthy Plate" and tell me what categories of intake they are lacking for that day. Our kids are surrounded by more than junk food; they are bombarded by crap-food (pardon me). Sometimes it's distressing, but all the more reason that we cannot give up the fight.

There's still time to make a difference and show our Lord that we really do value the very good creation He gave us.

DAY 8: FAITH EXERCISE

"Now faith is the assurance of things hoped for, the conviction of things not seen." Hebrews 11:1 (NASB)

Taking care of our bodies is a faith journey. When we take care of our bodies, we are inherently living by the principle presented in Hebrews 11. How? Because when we exercise, for example, we do not immediately see the results. We trust that the exercise we are doing today will have beneficial results in the future. We are trusting in the assurance of things hoped for when we work out. When we eat a well-balanced diet, we do not immediately see the good it does to our bodies. Instead, we trust that the food is doing good things inside of us, and perhaps we will eventually see the benefits on the outside. When we honor the bodies God has given us and care for them appropriately, we do so in faith that the efforts will be well worth it. It is a faith exercise.

The same is true with our spiritual disciplines, isn't it? When we read our Bibles each morning, we do so in faith and as a discipline. Yes, we might "feel" a little better after doing so (just as we might feel a little better after a workout), but the real hope is that the benefit will be much more far-reaching. When we build prayer and solitude and charity into our lifestyle, we do so with the hope that through it God will develop a more Christ-like person in us. And God promises that He will. The spiritual disciplines we incorporate into our lives might have momentary and immediate impact, but the real benefit is much more cumulative and long-term.

And so it is with the body.

So press on. Exercise the faith that is given to you. The faith we use in the physical realm is the same faith we use in the spiritual realm.

And trust that the One who began the good work in you is faithful to complete what He has begun.

DAY 9: TRAINING

"I press on ...." Philippians 3:14(a) (NIV)

Some days are like that. Certain seasons in life can be like that. And sometimes it seems that all of life is like that. Requiring me simply to press on.

Sports training and conditioning can be like that too. Whether it's for a triathlon, marathon, or plain-old health improvement ... some days we just need to press on. We need to make ourselves run the required miles for the day, swim and bike for the day, or simply just get up and go to the gym even when we don't feel like it. Why? Because we know it's all cumulative. We know that, ultimately, we are in pursuit of a bigger goal and that we might not reach it if we let today's feelings get in our way. We press on for the goal (... whatever it is).

Spiritually, we are in training too. Life on earth is a training ground for what is to come -- a victory that Christ has already won for us, and yet (in some inexplicable way) we partner in and participate in as we journey through life. We press on ... sometimes even when we don't feel like it ... because ultimately we want to prove ourselves grateful and worthy of all He has done for us. We want to be faithful to the One who created us and gave His all for us. We keep doing what He has told us is right and good (and avoiding the opposite), because He has told us it pleases Him. And we want to please Him.

So today, I press on. I press on, even though it's hard today. I press on because I know that one step forward and two steps backward is really one step in the wrong direction. I press on, as Paul says, "toward the goal to win the prize for which God has called me heavenward in Christ Jesus."

And I hope you press on too.

DAY 10: THE GIFT OF BODY

"Every good and perfect gift is from above, coming down from the Father of the heavenly lights, who does not change like shifting shadows. He chose to give us birth through the word of truth, that we might be a kind of first fruits of all He created."
James 1:17-18 (NIV)

When most of us hear that James 1:17, we think of people or blessings or opportunities or even material things, but do we ever think about the more basic and integral parts of our lives and realities? Food, shelter, air, water, breath? Even our bodies?

Whether you acknowledge it or not, your body is an amazing gift, given to you by your Heavenly Father. The human body can grow itself, heal itself, alert you of pain or injury or allergies. The human body has eleven very intricate and complex systems. The muscular system alone is amazing, not to mention the cardiovascular system, the respiratory system, the neurological system, etc. And the human eye alone is astounding in form and function! God gave people an incredible gift in these bodies; a gift of creation that God called "very good" *(See Genesis 1:31)*.

Do you see your body as very good? Do you treat it as something very good? Do you cherish it as a good and perfect gift from your Heavenly Father?

I give my kids gifts sometimes. I love my kids immensely, and I try to give them things I think they need or will enjoy. Suffice it to say that I know when they love the gift I have given, because they cherish and care for it. I also know when they don't.

As humans living in a world riddled with fallenness, some of us have ideas of what a "perfect" gift should look like -- an idea undoubtedly shaped, at least in part, by the fickle and unrealistic views of the culture around us. Others of us live more physically impacted by the world's fallenness, whether it is through disease or aging or tragedy. And cherishing the body becomes more challenging.

But the encouragement is this: our bodies are still amazing. God made your body and breathed His life into it. He sustains and renews your breath every day.

And God is not fickle or unrealistic, but constant and sure. So, as long as God gives us breath, let's thank Him and honor Him and praise Him for the gift of body . Let's learn to steward it well and care for it as someone who appreciates such a good gift!

DAY 11: ALL OF ME

"I will give thanks to You, for I am fearfully and wonderfully made! Wonderful are Your works, and my soul knows it very well." Psalm 139:14 (NASB)

Hanging in my exercise room, is a poster of the human body and all its various muscle groups. Each muscle group has a different color, and as you look at it, you cannot help but be awed by how intricate and complex it all is. How all the various muscle groups are interrelated and interdependent. I find it amazingly beautiful! And on this poster, I have placed a translation of Psalm 139:14 to constantly remind me of the amazing God who fashioned us with such care.

Sometimes when I look at it, I am reminded that this poster only represents the muscular system. There are other systems too, like our skeletal system, neurological system, lymphatic system, cardiovascular system, etc., etc. Layers upon layers of care and complexity! We truly are fearfully and wonderfully made.

So, with fear and wonder, I want to honor what God has so carefully fashioned. With fear and wonder, I want to care for this intricate mechanism He has fashioned for me. With fear and wonder, I want to thank God not just with my mouth, but with my whole being.

With fear and wonder, I am reminded that my physicality is intertwined with my spirituality. And I want to love God with all of me.

DAY 12: ATTENDING

"Then the man and his wife heard the sound of the Lord God as He was walking in the garden in the cool of the day, and they hid from the Lord God among the trees of the garden. But the Lord God called to the man, "Where are you?" Genesis 3:8-9 (NIV)

God's first plan was to have fellowship with those He created. From the start, God has desired to do life with those He created in His own image.

But sin interrupted that intimacy. And many things continue to interrupt our intimacy with God. At times, we often find ourselves hiding from God, ashamed or afraid, like Adam and Eve. Other times, we find ourselves too busy to stay connected to God, as there are so many other things pressing for our attention. And sometimes, we simply have to admit that we haven't really learned how to stay connected to God in the midst of everyday life activities. We haven't disciplined ourselves well

23

enough to be present with God while we do other things.

There's an old book called *Practicing the Presence of God* by Brother Lawrence. It's a short little book that beautifully describes the need to practice God's presence as we go about our day. (I'd highly recommend it if you haven't already read it. It's powerful ... & short!). Just like we need to practice different skills and exercises and moves, we also need to practice living amongst the presence of God. We need to practice being constantly aware of and in tune with His presence.

Working out has become one of those times for me. It is a time when I practice staying my inner mind on Him while my body and superficial thoughts are focused on my work out. It's a time when I practice attending to God while I am also attending to other things. When I work with clients, my intent is for them to attend (and for me to help them attend) both to God and to their workout.

It takes practice to get good at anything. It takes practice to attend to God. It takes practice to attend to God while also attending to other things. Seize the opportunities presented in working out to practice attending to God and to your workout. May it strengthen both your body and your soul.

DAY 13: POSTURE OF PRAYER

"O God, we meditate on your unfailing love as we worship in Your temple." Psalm 48:9 (NLT)

Many of us approach prayer as if it is our time to convince God to agree with us in our requests. And yes, there are a few Biblical examples of when a person's persistence in prayer alters the outcome. But more often than not, prayer is about getting me more in tune with God's perspective and God's will. Prayer is more about changing me. So an effective "posture" for entering time with God is a posture of openness and receptivity -- ready to listen and hear, laying our hearts before God and even more eager to hear His heart.

So when I enter exercise, I try to enter it in a posture of prayer -- ready to devote this time to Him ... to listen, to hear and to surrender my will to His. It's a time that I set aside to be with Him while I care for this body He gave me. Where, when I hit physical struggles and limitations, I am reminded

25

of my personal and spiritual struggles and limitations ... and I receive encouragement or admonishment or insight that I need from the One who made me.

For me, it's easiest to do this in the exercise space I've created in my basement, where I've hung posters and verses and can play my worship music. But even when I'm at the health club, I strive to maintain a posture of prayer. Open and ready to listen or respond to what He brings.

The body, mind and spirit are deeply intertwined. God made us that way. The exercise of one aspect of us is not and should not be isolated from the exercise of another. Try entering your workouts in a posture of prayer. I think you will find that He exercises more than just your body!

DAY 14: BREATHE

"The Spirit of God has made me; the breath of the Almighty gives me life." Job 33:4 (NIV)

One of the things I love about exercise is the constant reminder to breathe. Regardless of the type of exercise -- running, weight-lifting, yoga, etc. -- we constantly need reminders to breathe.

You'd think it would be intuitive to breathe, but for some reason, we tend to hold our breath when exercise gets tough. We clench and try to gut it out, and we forget to breathe.

Isn't that true in our spiritual journeys too? Isn't it true that when we feel things getting tough, we "hold our breath" and try to gut it out. We clench and dig deep and rely on ourselves and our own ability to get through. Why do we do that? Why, when the very thing we need to do is to breathe?

It is the breath of the Almighty that gives me life.

When "the Lord God formed man from the dust of the ground, He breathed into his nostrils the breath of life, and the man became a living being." (*Genesis 2:7 (NIV)*). It is His breath that gives me life, literally. In the New Testament, the Greek word used for breath ("pneuma") can also be translated "spirit" ... so I can also say that it is His Spirit that gives me life. Literally.

So when I breathe, I invite the Spirit in. When I breathe, I let go of the need to gut it out and make it on my own. When I breathe, I invite the Spirit in, and I surrender to His life-giving and sustaining power. The breath of the Almighty gives me life!

DAY 15: THE MAIN THING

"[P]hysical exercise has some value, but godliness is valuable in every way." 1 Timothy 4:8a (NET)

I've hardly been able to exercise for over a week now. My system has been fighting this awful cold virus, and working out too much would only exacerbate the problem. Not only do I miss the physical routine of exercise, but I also miss my worship time with God -- worshipping Him with all of me -- spirit, mind and body. But this week, caring for and stewarding this body God gave me means letting it rest and heal.

For some of us exercise enthusiasts, it can be hard to stop the routine when necessary and rest. For others, it might be hard to keep the focus on God and His glory, because focus can so easily be diverted to external outcomes and vanity.

And all of us need reminders to keep the main thing, the main thing. And the main thing, for all of us, is the "pursuit of knowing our Lord Jesus Christ more intimately" *(2 Peter 1:8 (NET))*.

That's what it's all about -- knowing our Lord Jesus more intimately and becoming increasingly more like Him so that we can reflect more of His glory in this world. Of course, there are many ways in which we can and should pursue godliness (or God-likeness). But regardless of our specific disciplines and practices, Scripture is clear that we must keep the goal of pursuing His likeness first and foremost in our pursuit.

So this week, as I struggle to care for and steward my body in a different way, I am reminded once again to keep the main thing the main thing. This week, I get to learn fresh ways of knowing Jesus more intimately. And when I am able again to worship God and commune with Him in one of my preferred ways, perhaps I will be able to reflect a little   more   of   His   glory.

DAY 16: REST-ORATION

"For in six days, the Lord made the heavens, the earth, the sea and everything in them; then He rested on the seventh day. That is why the Lord blessed the Sabbath day and set it apart as holy."
Exodus 20:11 (NLT)

Do you consider rest to be holy? Most of us don't. Our lives are crazy busy and overfilled. Silence is a rarity ... and rest? Well, rest is hard to come by.

From another perspective, however, perhaps our subconscious does know that rest **is** holy. Think about it: when someone has been "worked to death," it reveals a lack of respect for that person. Their personal value has been disregarded and minimized. To allow rest would be giving a level of respect.

Perhaps allowing rest denotes honor and respect to ourselves and to others.

Perhaps to rest means to quit working and chasing our tails and trust that God is in charge and will take care of us, because ... well ... He promises to. And we trust Him, right?

Let's consider allowing our bodies to rest because we trust in God and we value the bodies He has given us. So here are a few thoughts:

- Do you get enough **sleep**? Most adults do not. God gave us sleep and, on average, our bodies need at least 8 hours a night.
- Are you constantly on the go, running from one thing to another? If so, then your body, mind and soul are probably tired. Rest is key to restoration, so monitor your **pace of life**.
- Do you ever set time apart just to rest? I am a firm believer in keeping the **Sabbath** and in taking periodic solitude retreats. Honor your body, mind and soul by resting from all of life's craziness and reconnecting with yourself and with God.

God created a rhythm of life for us, and that rhythm includes rest. Maybe we too can rediscover the holiness of rest.

DAY 17: STRETCHING

"Enlarge the place of your tent, stretch your tent curtains wide, do not hold back; lengthen your cords, strengthen your stakes. For you will spread out to the right and the left; your descendants will dispossess nations and settle into desolate cities."
Isaiah 54:2-4 (NIV)

Recently, I've started teaching some stretching classes again. It's such a good practice to get into -- the intentional stretching and lengthening of muscles. One of the things I remind the folks in my class is that we lose flexibility as we age ... & as we lose flexibility, we lose mobility. Our joints are restricted from their optimal range of motion because the surrounding muscles are too tight to allow such motion. So by losing flexibility and then mobility, we become less able to respond to the demands life puts on us. To the extent I can help it, I don't want that to happen to my body.

And I don't want that to happen to my soul either.

Our souls can also become inflexible. We can get too comfortable, too set in our ways, too stiff, or too hardened and brittle to respond to God's call on our lives. We can refuse to lengthen and stretch and grow ... & by doing so, we can impede God's work not only in our lives but also through our lives to the world and others around us.

Just as I tell those attending my stretch class that it takes time and repetition to stretch tight muscle groups, I am reminded it also takes time and repeated intentionality to open up & allow God to do new things in me and through me. Just as it takes practice for muscle memory to develop and for muscles to expand, so it takes spiritual practices to allow God to stretch us in new ways and to new heights.

God has a wonderful plan for our lives. He has great things He is going to accomplish, and He wants to use us to do it! May we stay malleable and flexible enough to always respond to Him!

DAY 18: IT ALL STARTS HERE

"Your workmanship is marvelous -- how well I know it!"   *Psalm 139:14b (NLT)*

If only.

If only we knew it so well, our world would be a different place. For I believe Psalm 139 lies at the crux of our spiritual formation. And until the church can get it right, we cannot be our biggest and brightest to the rest of the world.

Psalm 139 talks about how intricately and intimately God made each of us and knows each of us. It speaks very practically about the love God has for us and how that love has been expressed in the wonderful creations that we are. *"You made all the delicate, inner parts of my body and knit me together in my mother's womb. Thank you for making me so wonderfully complex -- **how well I know it!**"* *(Ps. 139:13-14)*. And this isn't the only place God expresses this sentiment. One of my favorites is Ephesians 2:10, where we are called God's workmanship, God's masterpiece, God's *poiema* -- God's poem.

But we don't know it. By and large, we don't know that at our core. Because if we did, we would value ourselves differently. And if we valued ourselves differently, we would interact with ourselves differently. If I value the masterpiece that God made in me, I will honor it and care for it and learn to love it -- for no other reason that because God made it for me and gave it to me, and it is wonderfully made. And if you believed it, you might interact with yourself differently too.

I'm not talking about arrogance or self-love in that way. (Arrogance, by the way, is often a cover-up for insecurity, anyway.) I'm talking about a deep knowing that God created me carefully and thoughtfully, and that God loves me more than I can ever comprehend.

And once I **know** these truths -- that God made me a wonderfully complex masterpiece -- then I can start seeing and knowing *you* as a wonderfully complex masterpiece ... and I start interacting with *you* with more honor and dignity. And then the church, with each of us interacting with each other in such a way -- oh what a beauty the church would be!

But it all starts here. How well do you know the wonder of God's workmanship?

How much do you really believe that God loves you? How much do you really believe that you are God's poem?

DAY 19: RENEWAL

"Instead, let the Spirit renew your thoughts and attitudes. Put on your new nature, created to be like God -- truly righteous and holy." Ephesians 4:23-24 (NLT)

I was in yoga the other day, and I noticed how much my self-talk has shifted since I first started doing yoga. How much kinder and encouraging and understanding I was ... instead of criticizing and judging myself so much. The owner of the studio tells me she sees that all the time. She says when people start yoga, they often can't use the mirror to look themselves in the eye, but after a time they begin to reflect their own gaze. One of the first steps to self-acceptance – to be able to look upon yourself without critical judgment and critique.

There is a power to our thoughts and inner mental talk.

ABC News published an article in 2015 entitled **10 Rules Fit People Live By**. The essence of the article was that fit people focus on positive thinking -- they have trained their minds and attitudes toward the positive -- they have learned to control their thinking instead of letting their thinking control them. The article may or may not be scientifically valid, but it's interesting how the wisdom of the world sometimes echoes the wisdom of God, isn't it?

God has told us all along that there is great power in our minds. He tells us that in Ephesians, in Romans, and elsewhere. He tells us that our minds and thoughts and attitudes need to be renewed ... but instead of using worldly wisdom, God teaches that it's His Spirit and Scripture that needs to renew us. God's Spirit and the "cleaning of God's Word" are the optimal tools to renew our thoughts and attitudes. (*See Romans 12:1-2, Ephesians 4:23-24, Ephesians 5:25-26*).

So the next time you are working out, check your self-talk. Arm yourself with a verse or two to allow God's Spirit and Word to renew and refocus your mind. Consider praising Him because you ARE fearfully and wonderfully made (*Psalm 139:14*), or remember that you CAN do all things through Christ who strengthens you (*Philippians 4:13*), or claim the truth that you too are being made new (*Revelation 21:5*) and want to join in to the process. And may God renew your mind ... and your body and soul for His glory!

DAY 20: CHOOSING WISELY

"All things are lawful, but not all things are profitable." 1 Corinthians 10:23a (NASB)

We all gravitate towards the things we like ... the things that are easy for us ... the things we prefer. And we all tend to avoid the things we don't like ... the things that are hard for us ... the things that take more work. It's part of human nature. That's why Paul reminds us to choose wisely.

The same is true in regard to caring for our bodies. Maybe you are into eating well, but not into exercising ... or vice-versa. Perhaps you love cardio-training but not resistance training. Perhaps you are great at working your body but not at giving it the proper rest it needs. God gives us the freedom to choose -- to decide how we spend our time & energy in stewarding what He has given us. Yes, it is lawful for you to do your sixth cardio workout of the week ... but perhaps it would be more profitable to do some resistance training ... or even to rest your body. Yes, you can work out like a fiend and then go "reward" yourself with a burger & fries. But perhaps it would be more profitable to reward your body with what it really needs (like proteins, healthy fats, fruits & vegetables).

I was reading in **Jesus Calling** the other day, and it said: "The free will I bestowed on you comes with awesome responsibility. Each day presents you with choice after choice. Many of these decisions you ignore and thus make by default." (*Jesus Calling*, September 18) God allows me to make innumerable choices each day; unfortunately, I am not recognizing many of those opportunities as choices ... and therefore am not making the choices I should. I am giving away my choice to habit or thoughtlessness or other people (or worse).

And for so many of us, the **body** suffers as a result. The choices we make (or don't make) about what we are going to feed our bodies ... the choices we make (or don't make) about exercising and strengthening our bodies ... the choices we make (or don't make) about caring for and sanctifying our bodies. The many choices we make or don't make that cause our bodies to be unhealthy, undignified and unglorified. We, as a church, have forgotten to give our bodies to God. We, ironically called the *body* of Christ, have forgotten to make our bodies holy and acceptable to Him.

All things are lawful. But not all things are profitable. Choose wisely.

DAY 21: THINGS THAT REMAIN

"'Well done, my good and faithful servant! You have been faithful with a few things; I will put you in charge of many things. Come and share your master's happiness!'" Matthew 25:21 & 23 (NIV)

We all have struggles. We all have things that are difficult for us. Things that we wish were different. Things we wish we could change. One dear friend of mine has MS. Another dear friend has chronic insomnia. Another has breast cancer. We all have things we wish we could change.

I too have things in my life that I wish were different. And to those things, the Lord had a personal word for me yesterday. His word was this: *focus not on the things I have denied you; focus instead on the things I have given you, and steward them well.*

What's ironic about His Word to me is that it is very similar to the message I share all the time. My ministry is to remind people that God has given each of us an amazing gift called the body, and your own body is a gift to be cherished and cared for with its own unique crafting in mind. I'm constantly telling people that loving the body you have been given is a way to love the Giver -- a valid way to worship. That spending time and energy wishing it was different is not a response of gratitude, but love and stewardship is. And yet, in other ways, I find myself needing God's gentle reminder to *focus not on what He has denied me, but to focus instead on what He has given me, and steward it well.*

It can be hard sometimes. I have friends who are single and deeply want to be married. I have friends who are childless and deeply want children. I have friends whose kids have autism, another with a child who is partially paralyzed, and another whose child is battling brain cancer. It can be hard to keep our minds off of those things that He has denied ... but I know that if you asked each of my friends, they would, even still, acknowledge that God has been good to them ... particularly if they *focus not on that which God has denied them, but stay focused on what He **has** given them and work to steward it well.*

DAY 22: TRAINING GROUND

"The Lord is my strength and shield. I trust Him with all my heart. He helps me, and my heart is filled with joy. I burst out in songs of thanksgiving." Psalm 28:7 (NLT)

Hard times are training opportunities. Think of Joseph, who was sold into slavery by his brothers, taken to another country, imprisoned etc. (*See Genesis 37 ff*). What others intended for evil in his life, God used and intended for good (*Genesis 50:20*). God used seemingly disastrous events to train, prepare, and place Joseph in the right place at the right time for the right reasons. We all know the story ... but when it happens to us, it is hard for us to see and realize the chance to learn this principle for real and anew.

But challenging times are the perfect time to become acutely aware of and to grow our dependence on Him. As one author says: "Challenging times wake you up and amplify your awareness of needing My help." Challenging times forge our character. They also prepare the way for God to reveal His glory in greater ways.

So often, I am in training. And I am learning to embrace it. Ultimately, I want to know deep dependence on God. I want to trust in Him alone to save me. I want to see His glory revealed in my life like I have never seen it before. And so (when I have my wits about me) I train -- listening, watching, waiting, working, responding, obeying, trusting, and moving in faith.

As hard as it is sometimes – as tough as some training programs are – I want to be able to stand firm:

> The Lord is the strength of my life! Not anyone or anything else. The Lord God Almighty is my strength and my song! And with Him, I am victorious. No matter what.

Training ground *is* holy ground when we have Him to train us!

DAY 23: PERSONAL TRAINING

"O Lord, you examine me and know ...." Psalm 139:1 (NET)

Have you ever worked with a personal trainer? Someone who helps you customize your workouts to your specific lifestyle, tendencies and goal? If you get a good personal trainer and follow the program, you can see great results.

A good personal trainer will study you. They will learn your workout history, and they will learn about your injury history. They will study how your body adapts to training. They will discover how easily you build muscle, burn fat, grow in endurance, etc. They will see where your muscles are tight and where they are loose. They will help you discover where you are imbalanced and what needs to be corrected. They will also reveal your strengths and show you how to capitalize on those in beneficial and constructive ways. A good personal trainer gets to know the uniqueness of you so that he/she can help you get closer to your goals.

Said differently, a good personal trainer knows your story.

I have heard it said that, in Eastern thought, it is easier to experience God as an all-forgiving God. You see, in the Western part of the world, we tend to feel condemnation when we think of God as an all-knowing God. If God is omniscient, to us in the West, that means He knows all of my flaws, faults and mistakes. And that is true. But to a more Eastern-mindset, the fact that God is omniscient means that He knows my story. It means He understands me. The fact that He is all-knowing means, in fact, that He knows *all* about me. He knows why I struggle with the things I struggle with. He understands what brought me to that place. He sees it all. He knows why certain things hurt me the way that they do, because He saw it all. He walked through it with me. He already knows my underbelly, and He loves me anyway. He always has.

The truth is that because He is omniscient -- because He knows everything about me and my story -- He can sympathize and understand and love me no matter what. It is because He knows your story, because He understands you in detail, that He pursues you relentlessly and knows precisely how to restore and renew you.

The best personal trainer? Jesus. Simply Jesus. Omniscient, omnipotent Jesus.

DAY 24: HYDRATE

"Let anyone who is thirsty come to me and drink."
John 7:37b (NIV)

When we exercise, we sweat. Especially during
cardio-intensive training, we sweat a lot. And then
we need to hydrate. The more we sweat, the more
we need to hydrate. Common sense, right?

But the same principle applies to the rest of our
lives. The more we give out, the more we need to
replenish. The more we give away, the more we
need to make sure we refill ourselves. A friend of
mine calls it *soul care*. We cannot run on empty.
We need to come continually to the source of Living
Water and rehydrate.

During this season of life, I often feel the need to
rehydrate. As an introvert who is constantly with
my young children & play dates & church & small
groups, etc. etc., I feel tremendous need during this
season to prioritize time to care for my soul and to

come to Jesus and be filled with Living Water. For me, this season of life is like a super spin class during super humidity. I am sweating a lot! So, I'm trying to drink a lot of Water during this season.

I don't know what season you are in or what your temperament is, but I know that you need to hydrate. You need to hydrate everyday. If you are not "sweating" a lot this season, then perhaps the standard 64 ounces a day will do. But if you are sweating a lot, like I am, 64 ounces just won't do it.

If I were your trainer, I would remind you to hydrate after exercise; let me remind you to hydrate your soul as well!

DAY 25: THIRST

"I lift my hands to You in prayer. I thirst for You as parched land thirsts for rain." Psalm 143:6 (NLT)

Water is an amazing thing. An adult human is made up of at least 60% water, and every living cell in the human body needs water to keep functioning. Without water, a person can only survive a few days.

Have you ever been thirsty? I mean really thirsty? Perhaps you've gone on a major hike or attended a spin class without your water bottle? Or maybe you have run a long race and, after passing up one water station, eagerly anticipated the next one? Or maybe you've been dehydrated while sick, with your tongue stuck to the roof of your mouth (that feels more like a cotton field)?

Or maybe you've seen an animal or a person who has been deprived of water for such a long time that they need that water like it's their last breath?

Sometimes we need God like that.

Actually, we need God like that all the time ... but we don't *feel* the need for Him that acutely all the time. (Kind of like with water ....) At least that's how it is with me.

But the older I get and the longer I go on this journey, the more I learn that it **is God** I truly thirst for. From time to time, I turn to other things that appear to offer refreshment or replenishment. But it's a mirage. And I get frustrated, hurt and disappointed. And, every time, I am reminded that it is only God that can satisfy my thirst.

To find my refreshment from God Himself -- that is my true heart's desire. To thirst for Him -- the God of heaven and earth -- as a parched land thirsts for rain. And to thirst for Him all the time.

So I have placed Psalm 143:6 and Psalm 42:2 around some of the major water sources in my home. Particularly by the fridge in my gym. Because I want to be reminded, especially in those moments when I am hot and tired and recognize my thirst, that it is God for whom I really thirst.

DAY 26: THE AIR WE BREATHE

"This is what the Sovereign Lord says: 'Look, I am about to infuse breath into you and you will live. ... I will put breath in you and you will live. Then you will know that I am the Lord." Ezekiel 37:5-6 (NET)

Have you ever exercised until you were almost out of breath? Or maybe you have had the breath knocked out of you? If so, you have experienced the preciousness of breath.

Because otherwise, we take breath for granted. Breathing is as natural as, well, the air we breathe. And yet, when God formed mankind, He "formed the man from the soil of the ground and breathed into his nostrils the breath of life" (*Genesis 2:7*). Paul reiterates in the book of Acts that God Himself gives life and breath to everything and everyone (*Acts 17:25b*). And the writer of Ecclesiastes reminds us that when these bodies die, "life's breath returns to God who gave it" (*Ecc. 12:7b*).

Interestingly, the Hebrew word for breath in both Ezekiel 37 and in Ecclesiastes 12 is the word *ruach,* which can be translated either as "breath" or as "spirit." Just like the New Testament Greek word *pneuma* which also can be translated either as "breath" or "spirit."

Hmmmm.

Maybe the Spirit is as essential to our being as is breathing.

Maybe our very being is more integrated with God's being than we might image.

Maybe God is not closer than the air we breathe; maybe His Spirit IS the air we breathe.

Maybe when we breathe, we invite the Spirit of God in to give us life.

So the next time you are working out and begin to notice your breath, use it as a prompting to notice the Spirit. "Breathe in; Spirit in."

And the next time things get hard, and you are tempted to hold your breath -- breathe! Especially then, breathe.

When the resurrected Jesus appeared to His disciples, "He breathed on them and said to them, 'Receive the Holy Spirit'" (*John 20:21b-22*). May you also receive the Holy Spirit every moment of every breath.

DAY 27: TO HEAL

"This is the kind of fast I want. I want you to remove the sinful chains, to tear away the ropes of the burdensome yoke, to set free the oppressed, and to break every burdensome yoke." Isaiah 58:6 (NET)

Jesus came to heal, to set free, to redeem. The heart of the Almighty is to heal, to set free, to redeem – to release everyone from whatever "chains" keep them from achieving their fuller potential. And the Bible is emphatic that God is making all things new. *(See e.g., Rev. 21:5)*

What's cool to me is that our bodies were designed with the same objectives in mind. God made our bodies with His eternal attributes woven in. The bodies that God designed for us are, for example, designed to heal -- they are able to heal themselves from wounds or injuries inflicted upon them. The body, for example, is constantly renewing itself -- the skin renewing itself every 28 days, liver every 5 months, bones every 10 years, etc. God made our bodies in ways that reflect His amazing glory! Even though imperfect and aging, they nonetheless constantly reflect some of the glory of the One who made them.

And, by and large, the body does this automatically. Cells respond immediately to start forming blood clots, for example ... to bring extra blood and nourishment to the injured area... to swell and protect the injury ... to begin the healing process. No arguments, no negotiating, no denial. Just immediate action to heal and renew.

And thank God for that! Because (as evidenced by the other aspects of our lives), most of us would spend an inordinate amount of time denying that we have been hurt .... refusing to take the necessary steps and precautions ... and might even find ourselves totally out of commission as a result.

To be healed means you first need to admit you are hurting.

To be renewed means you first need to accept that you need renewing.

To be set free means you first have to acknowledge that you are truly in captivity.

To be redeemed means you first believe that you need a Redeemer.

May we see more fully the inherent beauty of being healed and renewed such that we eagerly embrace our brokenness. He IS making all things new. Will you join Him in His work in you?

DAY 28: LONG-TERM VIEW

"No discipline seems pleasant at the time, but painful. Later on, however, it produces a harvest of righteousness and peace for those who have been trained by it." Hebrews 12:11 (NIV)

You know what my least favorite part of parenting is? Disciplining my kids. It's really hard for me sometimes to go through the struggle, opposition, upsetness (is that a word?) and attacks that my kids can throw at me ...and all the while maintaining a calm and positive composure. But when I do it right, I am focusing on my **kids'** development (instead of my discomfort) and what's best for **them** long-term. I want them to learn the things that will benefit their future lives.

I wonder if that's how God feels when He disciplines us? Part of Him hates disciplining us, but He loves knowing what we can be in the long-term. He loves the fruit He sees in our lives when we are trained by it.

Exercise can be like that. Sometimes there are days we'd rather be anywhere else but working out, but the long-term view keeps us there. Just today, I was NOT in the mood for doing bicep curls, but hope for future benefits kept me there. The discipline of working out *is a faith exercise*.

God has formed so much of life to grow our long-term view. Exercise is one. Parenting is another. Faith, of course, is the ultimate one. Most of our journey on earth is aimed to grow us and form us and benefit us for eternity. Most of the journey is to prepare us for what is to come.

So how's your long-term view? Do momentary pains prevent you from long-term gains? Does immediate inconvenience keep you from future benefits?

I pray the promise of discipline for you and for me: to grow your long-term view ... and allow *all of yourself* to be trained by it.

DAY 29: PROCESS OF PURITY

"... Let us cleanse ourselves from everything that can defile our body or spirit. And let us work toward complete purity because we fear God."
2 Corinthians 7:1 (NLT)

If you ever wondered if God cared about the body, read Paul's letters to the church in Corinth. Paul's message is clear: It matters to God what we do with our bodies!

- God created our bodies, breathed life into them, and called His creation very good. (*Genesis 1:26-2:7*)
- In doing so, He has given each of us a unique and individual gift (our own body) to grow and steward and care for every day of our lives.
- And He made it clear that it matters to Him how we care for it. For example, to the nation of Israel, God gave many laws about what to eat, what not to eat; what to touch, what not to touch; when to work and when to rest. And for

the church, Paul echoes the principle of devoting all of who we are to the Lord -- that the body also matters in our devotion to God.

As I seek to raise the value of returning health and fitness to the realm of the sacred, I continually have to evaluate my own progress. As with the other aspects of ourselves that we devote to God (e.g., mind and soul), the process of devoting my body to God IS a journey. And real journeys generally do not go up and to the right all the time. Some seasons are better than others; some harder. Sometimes it's two steps forwards and one step back. Sometimes it's victory in one aspect with defeat in another. And my journey is the same. But God is constant.

So as you examine your life and your whole-life devotion, remember that God wants all of you. Don't stop at considering just what might defile your soul, but also ... as Paul reminds us ... what might defile the body as well. And when things go wrong (because they do), don't let the evil one use it to beat you down. Remember that God is the author of process ... that Jesus understands our weakness ... and victory has already been won for us (although we have yet to lay hold of it). Just get back up. Seek to learn what it is you need to learn, and never give up. In our weakness is His strength. We just need to find it.

"All of me, all for You."

That's the goal, but I fall down. And God in His love and mercy responds to my cries ... and lovingly picks me up and propels me forward.

Someday I'll get all the way there, but He will have brought me home by then. So until then, I'm in the process ....

DAY 30: VICTORY

"But the people who know their God will firmly resist ...." Daniel 11:32b (NIV)

Have you ever tasted victory? The thrill of achieving, of conquering, of overcoming? There's no other feeling quite like it. Knowing that you beat whatever it was and came out on top. Sweet victory!

But victory comes at a cost. Victory usually comes after hard work, serious investment and continued dedication. Any kind of race -- especially the big ones like a marathon, triathlon, or iron man -- requires tremendous training of the body *and* mind. Weeks and months of training, working through injuries and pain, learning to fuel the body properly, getting adequate rest, denying body and mind of things it might rather pursue in the moment, etc. Just completing the race is a victory of sorts ... and it comes at a cost.

Other parts of life are like that too. We all face trials and temptations of various kinds and sizes. Things that get in our way, make us stumble and fall, draw our eyes and our hearts away from the true and right things that (deep down) we really want. Sometimes the things that lure us are actually good things, but as the Lord says, they are not the best. (*See e.g., 1 Corinthians 6:12*). And the victory of saying "no" to the good-but-not-best -- while ultimately sweet – can hurt. Sometimes it hurts deeply.

Victory can be bittersweet.

I don't know what you are going through right now. I don't know where you are seeking victory (or where you may be tempted to admit defeat). But I can tell you that I understand. I can affirm that sometimes it hurts. A lot. I can also tell you that it is worth it ... that the Lord **will** provide a way out and the strength that you need. The God we know is waiting to supply what we need to resist. That doesn't mean it won't hurt, but it does mean that you will taste the (bitter)sweetness of victory. It does mean that you will feel the joy of the Lord's good pleasure upon you (as well as your own satisfaction that you did it).

So the next time you see a runner cross the finish line, with tears running down his face, collapsing in pain and relief ... remember the bittersweetness of victory. Remember the bittersweetness of God's own Ultimate Victory ... and praise the Lord for each and every victory He has enabled you to experience. And may that fuel you to continue pursuing victory-in-Christ in whatever your face.

ABOUT THE AUTHOR

Ashley Hall Roberts is the founder of Sh'maFit, a ministry devoted to returning health & fitness to the realm of the sacred. Combining 27+ years in the fitness industry with 10+ years of seminary studies and ministry, Ashley brings unique insight into what it means to love God with all of who we are -- *body*, mind, and spirit.

A certified Group Fitness Instructor and Personal Trainer, Ashley has been instructing for over 27 years. After leaving the practice of law, Ashley obtained her Masters degree from Trinity Evangelical Divinity School, summa cum laude, and has been on staff at various churches in the Chicagoland area. Ashley began her relationship with Christ as a camper at Kanakuk Kamps, which has shaped and greatly influenced her path and ministry.

Currently, Ashley teaches and leads various Sh'maFit classes, workshops and retreats across the country. She currently lives with her husband and two children in the suburbs of Chicago.

25039699R00041

Made in the USA
Columbia, SC
01 September 2018